Table of contents

Introduction to Voluntary Manslaughter

Voluntary manslaughter only applies where there is a murder charge. Murder is covered in the first booklet of *the law explained* series. However, I have repeated a little on *actus reus* and *mens rea* and a review of murder as a reminder. The main substance of this booklet is the two defences which reduce murder to manslaughter, loss of control and diminished responsibility.

Example

Jane stabs Jenny, who dies. This is murder. If Jenny had taunted Jane in some way, Jane may be able to use the defence of loss of control. If she is suffering from severe depression at the time, Jane may argue diminished responsibility. If either of the defences succeeds, Jane will be convicted of manslaughter, not murder. This is important because the mandatory life sentence for murder will not apply, which means that the judge can choose the sentence.

The tasks are intended to reinforce your learning so do these as you go along. The answers are at the end of the book. Some tasks will just ask you to jot down a few thoughts for use in an essay question, so there are no answers to these, but keep your notes for revision and exam practice. I have included occasional quotes so use these too; they show that you know what judges have to say about the law.

Criminal cases are usually in the form *R v the defendant*. It is acceptable to use just the name so if the case is **R v Miller** I have called it **Miller**. If another form is used, e.g., **DPP v Miller** I have used the full title, as you may want to look up the case for further information.

Civil cases are between the *claimant* and the *defendant*, although you will see the word *'plaintiff'* in cases before 1999.

There is a list of some common abbreviations in the appendix at the end of the book.

Chapter 1: Review of *actus reus, mens rea* and murder

Actus reus

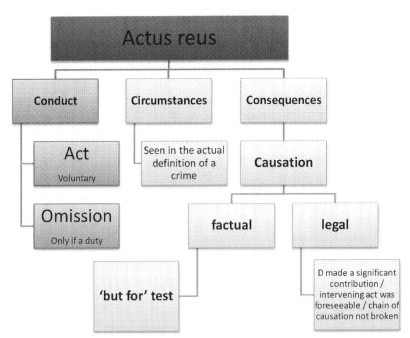

In most crimes, the act must be voluntary.

An omission, or failure to act, can amount to the *actus reus* if there is a duty to act. In all the following cases, a failure to act resulted in a death.

In **Pittwood 1902**, D had a contractual duty to shut the crossing so was guilty of manslaughter when he failed to do so.

In **Stone and Dobinson 1977**, a couple had a voluntary duty to care for a relative so were guilty of manslaughter for failing to do so. The same applies to murder.

In **Gibbins and Proctor 1918**, the D's had a duty to look after his daughter who lived with them. They intentionally omitted to give her food and the CA upheld their murder convictions.

In **Evans 2009**, D had created a dangerous situation by supplying drugs to her half-sister. She therefore had a duty to take steps to remedy the situation so was guilty of manslaughter for failing to do so.

Crimes where a particular consequence is part of the *actus reus* are called **result crimes**. For murder, death must result from (be caused by) D's act. The prosecution must prove causation both **factually** and **legally**.

Factual causation is proved using the 'but for' test. For murder the prosecution must show that 'but for' D's conduct, the victim would not have died.

Key case

In **White 1910**, D put cyanide in a drink intending to kill his mother, who was found dead shortly afterwards with the drink 3 parts full. In fact, the mother had died of a heart attack unconnected with the poison. The son was found not guilty of murder. He had the *mens rea* (he intended to kill her) but not the *actus reus* (his act didn't cause her death). He was guilty of attempted murder, however.

Legal causation is based on the 'chain of causation'. There must be an unbroken link, or chain, between D's action and the death. When something has occurred after D's original act, then it may be argued that the chain of causation is broken.

Key case

In **Cheshire 1991**, due to negligent treatment by the hospital, the victim of a shooting died. The court held that as long as D's action was a '**significant and operative**' cause of the death it need not be the sole cause. Hospital treatment will not break the chain unless it is "*so independent of D's acts and in itself so potent in causing death, that the contribution made by D is insignificant.*" Thus if D makes a significant contribution to the death this is enough, even if there are other causes as well.

The courts rarely allow medical treatment to break the chain of causation. The principle from **Cheshire** was followed by the CA in **Mellor 1996**, where failure to give proper treatment contributed to the death of the victim of an attack, but D was found guilty of his murder.

In **Pagett 1983**, D fired a shotgun at armed police while holding a girl hostage in front of him. They returned fire, killing the girl. The court held that the actions of the police did not break the chain because shooting back was a 'natural consequence' of his having shot first. This is based on the principle from **Roberts 1971** that a foreseeable act does not break the chain. In **Roberts**, D assaulted a girl who then jumped out of a moving car, and was injured. It was held that only if it was something that no reasonable person could foresee would the chain of causation be broken by the victim's actions. In **Williams & Davis 1992**, the CA said that the chain of causation is not broken unless V does something "*so daft or unexpected*" that no reasonable person could foresee it.

Essay pointer

If you were on the jury, would you know what acts should be considered 'independent' or 'potent' enough to break the causation chain? How significant must D's act be? What amounts to a 'daft' act by the victim? There may be a thin line between doing 'something wrong in the agony of the moment' and doing something 'daft'.

Coincidence of *actus reus* and *mens rea*

Actus reus and *mens rea* must coincide; however the court may view the *actus reus* as continuing or as a 'series' of acts.

In **Fagan v Metropolitan Police Commissioner 1969**, D accidentally drove onto a police officer's foot and then refused to move. The court held there was a continuing act (*actus reus*) up until the refusal to move (*mens rea*) therefore the two coincided.

In **Thabo Meli 1954**, the Ds tried to kill a man and rolled his body over a cliff. As it happened, he wasn't dead and the actual cause of death was exposure. The Ds argued that the first act (the attack), although done with *mens rea,* was not the cause of death (so no *actus reus*). The second act (pushing him over the cliff) was the cause of death, but was not accompanied by *mens rea* as they thought he was already dead. The court said that it was "*impossible to divide up what was really one series of acts in this way*".

The 'thin skull' rule

The chain is not broken by a particular vulnerability in the victim. Lawton LJ said in **Blaue 1975**, "*those who use violence on other people must take their victims as they find them*". Also known as the 'thin-skull rule', it means that if a particular disability in the victim makes them more likely to die,

D is still liable. The 'disability' is usually physical (like a pre-existing medical condition such as a 'thin skull') but in **Blaue** it was the fact that she was a Jehovah's Witness and so refused to have a blood transfusion.

Mens rea

The term *mens rea* refers to the state of mind of the accused at the time the *actus reus* is committed. As we saw *mens rea* and *actus reus* must exist at the same time.

The two main types of *mens rea* are intention and recklessness. Only the first applies to murder.

It is important to be able to identify both the *actus reus* and the *mens rea* of the offence when answering a problem question. Each and every part of a crime has to be proved beyond reasonable doubt (as we saw in **White**, if all the elements are not proved D is not guilty of the offence).

Many cases dealing with intention are homicide cases because intention differentiates murder from manslaughter. The *mens rea* for murder is an intention to kill or seriously injure someone. Intention can be direct or oblique (indirect).

Direct Intent

Direct intent means the result is D's aim or purpose. This is what most of us would understand by intention. If you pick up a loaded gun and fire it at someone with the aim of killing them, it can be said without any difficulty that you intended to do so. Intention was defined in **Mohan 1975** as 'the decision to bring about' the result, or prohibited consequence, whether that result was desired or not. The courts have given the concept of intention a wider meaning, however. This is referred to as oblique, or indirect, intent.

Oblique or indirect intent

Here the consequence isn't D's aim but is 'virtually certain' to occur because of D's actions.

The law on oblique intent was clarified somewhat by the HL in **Woollin 1998**, which confirmed the standard direction for the jury given by the CA in **Nedrick 1986**. This was:

> That death or serious bodily harm was a **virtual certainty** as a result of the defendant's actions and

> **the defendant appreciated** that such was the case

Essay pointer

The **Draft Code** definition is that D acts intentionally with respect to a result *"when he acts either in order to bring it about or being aware that it will occur in the ordinary course of events"*. In **Woollin**, Lord Steyn referred to the **Draft Code** but thought the **Nedrick** test was "very similar". It is arguable that the HL should have adopted the code if they thought it so similar. It seems quite clear and would become the law if the **Code** were ever adopted.

Examination tip

When applying the law you need only use **Nedrick** and **Woollin**, and only then in cases of oblique intent, not where it is direct. This was made clear in **Woollin**. D's knowledge will be an important factor. Look carefully at the facts for information such as 'they knew that ...' or 'unknown to them ...'. These comments will help you to decide whether intent is direct or indirect and to apply the test if necessary.

Transferred Malice

Mens rea can be transferred from the intended victim to the actual victim. This means that if you intend to hit Steve but miss and hit Joe you cannot say 'but I didn't intend to hit Joe so I had no *mens rea*'. In **Latimer 1886**, D aimed a blow at X with his belt but missed and seriously wounded V. He had the intent (*mens rea*) to hit X, and this intent was transferred to the wounding (*actus reus*) of V. Thus, he had both the *mens rea* and the *actus reus* of wounding. If V had died the charge could have been murder. However, the *actus reus* and *mens rea* must be for the *same* crime.

Murder

The rules on voluntary manslaughter only apply where there is a charge of murder. Here is a very brief summary of murder.

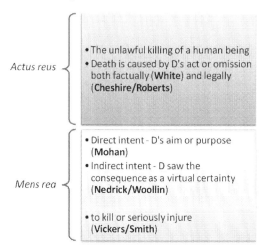

Actus reus
- The unlawful killing of a human being
- Death is caused by D's act or omission both factually (**White**) and legally (**Cheshire/Roberts**)

Mens rea
- Direct intent - D's aim or purpose (**Mohan**)
- Indirect intent - D saw the consequence as a virtual certainty (**Nedrick/Woollin**)
- to kill or seriously injure (**Vickers/Smith**)

Many examination questions require a discussion of the above issues on *actus reus*, *mens rea* and murder as well as voluntary manslaughter, because murder must be proved before considering the special defences which make it manslaughter. Now we will look at those special defences to a charge of murder which will lead to a conviction for manslaughter instead.

Chapter 2: Voluntary manslaughter under the Coroners and Justice Act 2009 – Loss of control

> *"... the reasonable man is a fixed rather than a variable creature. The yardstick is a person of the age and sex of the appellant having and exercising ordinary powers of self-control."*

Lord Justice Scott Baker in **Mohammed 2005**

Loss of control replaces the previous defence of provocation. The law is now found in **s 54** and **s 55** of the **Coroners and Justice Act 2009** which came into force in October 2010.

S 54 states:

> *'(1) Where a person ("D") kills or is a party to the killing of another ("V"), D is not to be convicted of murder if —*
>
> *(a) D's acts and omissions in doing or being a party to the killing resulted from D's loss of self-control,*
>
> *(b) the loss of self-control had a qualifying trigger, and*
>
> *(c) a person of D's sex and age, with a normal degree of tolerance and self-restraint and in the circumstances of D, might have reacted in the same or in a similar way to D.'*

The **Coroners and Justice Act 2009** repealed **s 3** of the **Homicide Act** and changed the name of the defence to loss of control. You will come across the previous defence of provocation in cases prior to 2010, and some of the old law still applies.

The burden of proof is on the prosecution. If D raises loss of control as a defence, then the prosecution must prove beyond reasonable doubt – the criminal standard of proof – that the case is *not* one of loss of control. (With the alternative defence to murder of diminished responsibility, the burden is reversed and D must prove the defence.)

Examination tip

Remember these defences ONLY apply to a murder charge. Don't try to apply them to other crimes. Where there is a death combined with intent to kill you can deal with the murder issues and then look at these defences. If intent and causation are clear, you don't need to discuss these in detail. Move quickly to the defences having briefly explained why the charge is likely to be murder. Only if the facts indicate it is necessary, for example, if there is a possible break in the chain of causation, or if intent may be hard to prove, should you discuss these. Examiners know you cannot discuss everything in the time so questions are usually set which address specific issues. Be selective!

Under **s 54**, for the defence to succeed, there are three questions to consider:

> *did D lose self-control?*
>
> *was the loss of self-control triggered by something specified in s 55?*
>
> *would a normal person of D's sex and age have reacted in the same way in D's circumstances?*

Did D lose self-control?

S 54(1) states:

> *'D's acts and omissions in doing or being a party to the killing resulted from D's loss of self-control'*

Note the words 'resulted from'. This means the killing must have been caused by the loss of self-control; this is a new requirement under the **2009 Act**.

Whether D lost self-control is a matter for the judge. If there is evidence of loss of control the judge will put it to the jury to decide on the facts whether D did lose self-control and whether the killing resulted from this, and may do so even if D does not raise it as a defence. This was seen in **Thornton 1992**, discussed below.

Under the old law, the loss of control had to be 'sudden and temporary'. In several cases women who had suffered years of abuse killed their partners. Accused of murder, they argued the provocation defence. Many failed on the 'sudden and temporary' point because there was a 'cooling-off' period between the provocative conduct and the killing. Under **s 54(2)** there is no longer a need for the loss of control to be sudden so these cases could succeed now. However, it may be difficult to prove any loss of control after a cooling off period.

Key case

In **Thornton 1992 and 1996**, Sara Thornton had gone to the kitchen to calm down after a violent argument. Whilst there she picked up a knife and sharpened it. She then went to where her husband was lying on the sofa and stabbed him. She didn't raise provocation at her original trial but the judge put it to the jury and it was rejected. The evidence was that she had cooled down by the time she stabbed him. Her conviction for murder in 1990 was upheld by the CA in 1991. In a later appeal in 1995 fresh medical evidence was introduced which showed she had a personality disorder and 'battered woman syndrome'. The CA held that the jury should have been allowed to consider whether a reasonable woman with these characteristics would have acted as Mrs Thornton did. However, Lord Taylor said that D "*cannot succeed in relying on provocation unless the jury consider she suffered or may have suffered a* sudden and temporary *loss of self-control at the time of the killing*".

A retrial was ordered. This took place in the Crown Court in May 1996 and she was convicted of manslaughter due to diminished responsibility (see next Chapter).

(I have included the dates as this case and its various appeals and retrials may seem confusing. 1992 and 1996 are the dates the case was reported (All England Law Reports).)

It is possible that she would now succeed with the loss of control defence, but unlikely. Although there is no longer a 'sudden and temporary' requirement, there must be a loss of control, and she does not appear to have lost control at all; she went into the kitchen to calm down before getting the knife. The Law Commission had advised not keeping the loss of control requirement and this is understandable considering the need to extend the defence to 'battered women' cases such as **Thornton**.

In **Ahluwalia 1992**, D set fire to her husband's bed when he was asleep. The defence of provocation again failed on the 'sudden and temporary' point, and again could still fail as she waited until he was asleep, so arguably did not lose control.

NB: At both subsequent retrials, the defence of diminished responsibility succeeded so these cases are relevant to both partial defences to murder.

There must be loss of *control* not just *self-restraint*. In **Cocker 1989**, D had finally given way to his wife's entreaties to ease her pain and end her life. His defence failed as the evidence showed he had not lost control. This would still apply for the new law.

Two differences with the law under the **Coroners and Justice Act 2009** are that:

S 54(2) states that the loss of self-control does not need to be sudden

S 54(4) states that the defence is not allowed if D acted in a 'considered desire for revenge'

Revenge is usually carried out after a period of time, so the defence could have failed under the sudden and temporary rule in the old law, now it would fail because revenge is excluded by the Act.

In **Ibrams and Gregory 1981**, the Ds and a girl had been terrorised by V. They planned to entice V to the girl's bed and then the Ds would attack him. They carried out the planned attack several days later, and killed V. At their appeal against a conviction for murder, the CA held that the defence failed because there was no sudden loss of control; the attack was planned and carried out over several days. Under **s 54(2)**, although there is no need for the loss of self-control to be sudden, any such time delay may indicate that there was no loss of control at all. It could also indicate a 'considered desire for revenge' and so be excluded by **s 54(4)**. Finally, it may fail because even if there was a loss of control at the start, it is unlikely to have caused D to kill several days later, so the killing did not 'result from' the loss of control as required by **s 54(1)**.

Another case relevant to these issues is **Baillie 1995**. In **Baillie**, D's son was getting drugs from a dealer who had threatened him with violence. When D found out, he drove to the dealer's house armed with a razor and a sawn-off shotgun. They had an argument and D shot the dealer as he left, killing him. The trial judge refused to allow the defence (then provocation) to be put to the jury and D appealed. The CA allowed the appeal because there was sufficient evidence for the matter to be put to the jury. This case could go either way now. There is no need for the loss of control to be sudden, but there is an element of revenge in D's act of driving to the dealer's house in response to the threat to his son. Much would depend on whether the jury saw it as a 'considered' desire for revenge. In **Baillie**, unlike in **Ibrams**, D drove to V's house whilst still angry, so any desire for revenge may not be deemed 'considered', also the killing could have 'resulted from' the loss of control as there was not a long gap between the two.

In one of three appeals heard together under the new Act, **Evans 2012**, the loss of control defence was considered. D had killed his wife after she had goaded him. He said she had stabbed him, but it was not clear if this was true, or whether he had done it himself. The prosecution case was that he killed her because she told him that she was going to leave him. The defence case was that she had stabbed him, and he had lost control and stabbed her. The main issue was whether he had 'acted in a considered desire for revenge'. The judge summed up in accordance with the Act and said:

> *"If you conclude so that you are sure either that this was a considered act of revenge by the defendant or that he had not lost the ability to control himself, this defence does not apply and your verdict would be guilty of murder".*

He was found guilty of murder. The CA dismissed his appeal (heard together with **Clinton** and **Parker**, see below) and held that there was sufficient evidence that he had acted in revenge so the jury decision was correct. The judge had summed up both the prosecution and defence arguments as regards the possibility of it being an act of revenge, so the conviction was fair.

Was the loss of self-control triggered by something specified in s 55?

Another difference with the new law is that under **s 54(1)(b)** there must be a 'qualifying trigger'. This refers to whether something triggered D's loss of control – and what that something was. Under the old law, there was no specific restriction on what caused D to lose control.

S 55(1) of the Act sets out the qualifying triggers. The loss of control must be triggered by:

> *D's fear of serious violence from V against D or another identified person; or*

> *a thing or things done or said (or both) which —*

> *(a) constituted circumstances of an extremely grave character, and*

(b) caused D to have a justifiable sense of being seriously wronged.

Or a combination of both of these

So what will amount to a qualifying trigger? Fear of serious violence suffices, e.g., reacting to someone threatening to attack you, as long as 'serious' violence is feared. The defence may succeed where it failed before, in the case of women who fear violent abuse, as long as it causes a loss of control.

The violence need not be directed at D. In **Pearson 1992**, a boy killed his father because of the father's ill treatment, not of himself but of his brother, and the defence succeeded. This is still the case; fear of violence against D or *'another identified person'* will be enough. The 'things done and said' means the loss of control can be caused by both actions and words. Again, this is the same as the previous law. In **Doughty 1986**, the crying of a baby was said to amount to what was then called provocation.

It is questionable whether **Doughty** would succeed now. This is because the 'things done or said' must be 'extremely grave' and 'justifiably' cause D to feel 'seriously' wronged. The crying of a baby is unlikely to be deemed *extremely grave* nor is a jury likely to be persuaded that it caused D to have a *justifiable* sense of being *seriously* wronged.

In **Parker 2012**, D had killed his wife during an argument. The evidence was that he had placed knives close to hand in preparation for the attack. However he argued that he had 'lost it' when she told him she didn't love him. The judge summed up the new law to the jury as follows:

'When D stabbed his wife had he lost self-control?

If not then go no further. Otherwise, consider whether his loss of self-control was caused by a qualifying trigger. The qualifying triggers are things said or done by his wife which

a. constitute circumstances of an extremely grave character and

b. caused the defendant to have a justified sense of being seriously wronged.

If neither was the case then he is guilty of murder, otherwise consider whether a man of D's age with a normal degree of tolerance and self-restraint would have reacted in the same or in a similar way to the way that the defendant reacted'.

The jury reached a verdict of murder. In dismissing D's appeal (heard with **Clinton** below) the CA held that the matters relied on by D could not reasonably be treated by any jury as circumstances of an extremely grave character which caused him to have a justifiable sense that he had been seriously wronged.

The Act specifically excludes sexual infidelity as a qualifying trigger. Under the old law, it would have been allowed as a cause of the loss of control. In fact the original law was introduced to cover such cases. Under **s 55(6)**, if the thing 'done or said' constituted sexual infidelity it is to be disregarded.

In **Holley 2005**, (discussed below) D killed his girlfriend with an axe after she had slept with another man; she had also taunted him about his lack of courage. The fact that she had slept with someone else would be irrelevant as sexual infidelity is excluded by **s 55(6)** but the taunt about his lack of courage would be 'a thing said' so would be relevant.

Key case

In the third of the three cases heard together, **Clinton 2012**, D had killed his wife during a heated exchange and claimed both diminished responsibility and loss of control. She had told him she was having an affair and he had seen graphic pictures of her and her lover on Facebook. The couple also had financial difficulties and were undergoing a trial separation. The evidence was that he had planned the death having done some research on the internet. The jury rejected the diminished responsibility plea and the judge held that there was no loss of control due to one of the 'qualifying triggers' as required by the **Coroners' and Justice Act**, and also that the wife's infidelity should be ignored as this was specifically excluded by the Act. He was convicted of murder and appealed. The CA held that the judge had misdirected herself about the possible relevance of the wife's infidelity. Under **s 54(1)(c)** regard should be had to 'the circumstances of D'. The CA said this meant all the circumstances should be taken together. In this case, the sexual infidelity was an essential part of the whole, and had had sufficient impact on D to suggest the defence should have been put to the jury. A retrial was ordered.

Also excluded under **s 55(6)** are situations where D has incited either the fear of violence or the thing done or said, in order to have the excuse to use violence.

Example

Alan gets into an argument with Imran and says, "Come on then, come and do your worst." Imran then attacks Alan and Alan is now scared, he loses control and picks up a poker and hits Imran with it, killing him. Can Alan rely on loss of control if charged with murder? The answer is no, because he incited Imran to cause the fear of violence.

Essay pointer

In **Thornton**, the trial judge directed the jury on provocation and then added "... *it may be difficult to come to the conclusion that that was, and I use the shorthand, a reasonable reaction*". He then went on to suggest it wasn't reasonable to stab someone when "*there are other alternatives available, like walking out or going upstairs*".

Do you think his comments influenced the jury too much? Many people say abused women should simply walk away but life is rarely simple. Arguably, issues of fact like this should be left to the jury alone.

The question the jury had to ask themselves in **Thornton** was whether a reasonable woman would have done the same in her position, which brings us to the last point.

Would a normal person of D's sex and age have reacted in the same way in D's circumstances?

This is similar to the law as stated in **Holley**, but made a little clearer by the Act

S 54(1)(c) asks whether '*a person of D's sex and age, with a normal degree of tolerance and self-restraint and in the circumstances of D, might have reacted in the same or similar way*'. This is further clarified by **s 54(3)** which allows for '*reference to all of D's circumstances other than those whose only relevance to D's conduct is that they bear on D's general capacity for tolerance or self-restraint*'. This means age and sex are relevant in deciding the level of control expected and what the 'reasonable person' would do, but the addition of 'in the circumstances' means others matters can be looked at for the latter as long as they don't relate to D's capacity for self-restraint. A medical problem like an addiction, or a history of abuse would be a 'circumstance' but a short temper would not because this relates to D's capacity for restraint.

Many of the old cases will still be relevant and will anyway be needed for evaluation and discussion of reforms.

The question is objective, what 'a person' would do, not what D did. The Act refers to these persons having the same age and sex as D. What other personal characteristics can be attributed to this hypothetical person has caused many problems over the years. In **Camplin 1978**, a 15 year-old boy hit V with a chapatti pan after being homosexually assaulted and then taunted about it. V died and D was charged with murder. The HL said the question was whether a reasonable person of his *age* and *sex* would have done as he did. The **2009 Act** confirms this.

It was not fully clear from **Camplin** whether characteristics other than age and sex could be taken into account. Earlier cases centred on physical characteristics; this was later extended to mental ones. One of the reasons for ordering a retrial in **Thornton** was that this development had occurred since her original trial. In addition, the characteristics had to be both *relevant* and *permanent*. In **Newell 1980**, alcoholism was a possible characteristic but was not allowed, as it wasn't related to the taunt, which was about his girlfriend. The fact that he was drunk wasn't attributable because it was a temporary state. The court asked the jury the question in the opening quote.

In **Morhall 1995**, glue sniffing was said by the CA not to be a characteristic to be attributed to the reasonable man but this was reversed by the HL. It was held that as D was addicted this would be attributable, in the same way that alcoholism is, but being drunk isn't. D had been taunted by V about his addiction and they got into a fight, during which he stabbed V.

In **Luc Thiet Thuan 1996**, the Privy Council took a more restrictive view. D killed his girlfriend after she teased him about his sexual prowess. There was evidence he was mentally unstable and had difficulty controlling his impulses. The Privy Council held that such mental factors could not be attributed to the reasonable man.

However, in **Smith 2000**, the HL widened the law again. D and a friend, both alcoholics, spent the evening drinking. D accused the friend of stealing his work tools and selling them to buy drink. They argued and D picked up a kitchen knife and stabbed his friend to death. At his murder trial, he argued provocation and said the jury should take into account the fact that he had been suffering from severe depression which reduced his powers of self-control. The judge rejected this argument but the HL accepted D's appeal. Lord Hoffman said that if the jury thought that there was some characteristic which affected the degree of control which society could reasonably have expected of him, it would be unjust not to take that into account. However, he did carry on to say that characteristics such as jealousy and obsession should be ignored, and Lord Clyde added 'exceptional pugnacity or excitability'.

So, this hypothetical person seemed to be getting quite a number of possible characteristics. In **Smith** Lord Hoffman referred to "monsters" being produced by attributing characteristics like glue sniffing to the reasonable person. The decision was only by a 3/2 majority. In particular, Lord Hobhouse produced a lengthy and reasoned argument against the decision. **Smith** is no longer likely to be good law; see **Holley** below where it was disapproved. The old law will be useful for evaluation questions though. The need for reforms and how far the Act has addressed the problems can be discussed.

Essay pointer

That this has been a problematic defence is clear. In 2003, the Law Commission said, "*its defects are beyond cure by judicial development of the law*". Some improvements are made in the **Coroners and Justice Act** but it is still complicated. Groups such as Justice for Women have long argued that the defence of provocation favours men as it can be used only by those strong enough to fight back. The women who suffer years of abuse and finally kill in desperation – but not in the heat of the moment – failed on the 'sudden and temporary' requirement. The removal of the need for a 'sudden and temporary' loss of control is an improvement but there must be a loss of control and the killing must result from this, so many of these cases would still not succeed. . The fact that loss of control must be shown goes against the Law Commission's proposals and prevents the defence clearly extending to cases of abuse against women, who may be physically weaker and liable to even greater abuse if they lose control and fight back.

The Privy Council looked at the issue again in **AG for Jersey v Holley 2005**. Although this was an appeal from a trial in Jersey, decisions of the Privy Council are highly persuasive on English law because the judges are Law Lords.

Key case

In **Holley 2005**, D, who was an alcoholic, killed his girlfriend with an axe whilst drunk. She had slept with another man and had also taunted D about his lack of courage. The CA substituted his conviction for murder for one of manslaughter, on the basis that the jury was misdirected on provocation. The prosecution appealed to the Privy Council, who held that **s 3** of the **Homicide Act** provided that provocation should be judged by one standard, not a standard that varied from D to D. **Smith** was held to be wrong on this point. D was to be judged against the standard of a person having 'ordinary powers of self-control', not against the standard expected of a particular D in the same position. Alcoholism is therefore no longer a 'relevant matter' for the jury when deciding whether a reasonable person would have done what D did. Note that Lord Hoffman dissented, but as his was the leading judgement in **Smith**, this is not surprising. It would seem that the law is back to **Luc Thiet**.

In **James; Karini 2008**, the CA followed **Holley** and disapproved **Smith**. It was noted that although decisions of the Privy Council are only persuasive, in **Holley**, the Council had consisted of nine law Lords so it was clear that in any appeal to the HL the decision would be the same.

The **Coroners and Justice Act** is similar to **Holley** and clarifies the circumstances to be taken into account in deciding whether 'a person' would have acted in a similar way to D. **S 54(1)** states that D is to be judged against a person of the same age and sex, having ordinary levels of tolerance and self-restraint in the circumstances of D. **S 54(3)** further adds that "the circumstances of D" is a reference to all of D's circumstances other than those whose only relevance to D's conduct is that they bear on D's general capacity for tolerance or self-restraint.

We saw that in **Newell 1980**, alcoholism was a possible characteristic, but was not allowed as it wasn't related to the taunt, and being drunk wasn't allowed because it was a temporary state. The Act will apply in a similar way. If he had been taunted about his alcoholism that could be one of the 'circumstances of D'; his drunkenness in itself would be ignored as this merely relates to his capacity for self-restraint.

In **Asmelash 2013**, D had been drinking with another man and got into a fight, during which D stabbed and killed him. He said the deceased had made him so angry that he lost control. The judge applied **s 54** of the **Coroners and Justice Act 2009** and said the jury should consider whether a person of D's sex and age with a normal degree of tolerance and self-restraint and in the same circumstances, but unaffected by alcohol, would have reacted in the same or similar way. D was convicted and appealed. The CA agreed with the judge that the consumption of alcohol should be ignored. The judges noted that in **Dowds 2012** (see next chapter), the new law was held not to change the rule that voluntary intoxication was not capable of establishing diminished responsibility. It was "inconceivable" that different criteria should apply to voluntary drunkenness depending on whether the partial defence under consideration was diminished responsibility or loss of control. This did not mean D could not use the loss of control defence; it simply means that the defence had to be approached without reference to the voluntary intoxication.

A quick summing up

Would a person of D's age and sex have reacted in the same way?

The level of control expected is that of a person of the same age and sex with normal levels of self-restraint. This is an objective test.

In the circumstances of D

This is partly subjective, D's particular circumstances, such as a history of abuse or alcoholism, can be taken into account, because these will relate not to the ability to retain control but to the reason for losing it. According to **Clinton**, sexual infidelity can be taken into account at this point as it affects the gravity of the circumstances as a whole, and their impact on D.

Other than those whose only relevance to D's conduct is that they bear on D's general capacity for tolerance or self-restraint

Things that made D lose control more easily, such as being drunk or aggressive by nature, will be irrelevant.

In **Mohammed 2005**, D found a young man in his daughter's bedroom. The man escaped but D killed his daughter with a knife. He was very strict and had a reputation for being violent and short-tempered. D was convicted of murder and appealed. The CA had to decide whether his violence and short-temper were relevant to the question of how a normal person would have reacted. Lord Justice Scott Baker said that D's temperament was not relevant and that

> "... the reasonable man is a fixed rather than a variable creature. The yardstick is a person of the age and sex of the appellant having and exercising ordinary powers of self-control."

This is similar to the new law. Violence and short-temper would relate to D's capacity for self-restraint or control, so cannot be taken into account when deciding whether a person would have reacted in a similar way.

Similarly, in **Luc Thiet Thuan 1996**, the evidence that he was mentally unstable and had difficulty controlling his impulses would not be taken into account. It is not clear whether the taunts about his sexual prowess would constitute circumstances of an 'extremely grave character' (and so be a qualifying trigger) but if so then they may be considered as a 'circumstance'. Following **Clinton**, it is unlikely these should be excluded even if they amounted to sexual infidelity.

It seems clear that things like a violent nature, short-temperedness, glue-sniffing, taking drugs or being drunk will be irrelevant as these affect D's capacity for tolerance and self-restraint. It is likely that (as in **Newell**) the 'particular circumstances that D was in' would have to be relevant to the loss of control, i.e., be a reason for the reaction. This was previously referred to as affecting the *gravity* of the provocation, rather than the *capacity for self-control*, and it would be similar under the new law.

Example

I am very embarrassed about a big growth on my back. Recently the doctor told me I needed an operation and I am very depressed and upset. Whilst drinking in the kitchen at a party someone calls me a hunchback. I pick up a large knife and stab them. I am charged with murder and plead loss of control.

There is evidence of 'things said', and I clearly lost control, but would a reasonable person have acted as I did? The jury will have to decide whether a person of my age and sex, with a normal degree of tolerance and self-restraint, would have done the same in my circumstances. My growth is a circumstance which can be taken into account as it affects the gravity of the comment, i.e., its effect on me. A person with no growth wouldn't be upset by the comment, so it is fair that this circumstance is taken into account. My drunkenness would not be allowed as it bears on my capacity for tolerance or self-restraint.

Following **Holley** and the **Coroners and Justice Act** my depression may not be allowed as a circumstance. I am not taunted about this so it is not likely to be seen as a relevant circumstance (it does not affect the gravity of the taunt or its effect on me), it is more likely to be seen as only it affecting my capacity for tolerance or self-restraint.

In the guidelines to the Act put out by the Ministry of Justice an example is given of a 23- year old woman who has killed her partner, who has beaten her frequently. It says the jury must consider whether a woman of that age with that history and with an ordinary level of tolerance and self-restraint might have done the same or a similar thing to their partner.

Task 1

Go to the Law Commission's website and see what they say concerning murder in 'completed projects' or 'publications'. You will find lots of information which you can refer to in an essay. You can see how far the **Coroners and Justice Act** took up the LC's suggestions. Quotes and discussions from this will help and will enhance an essay so make some notes and keep these for revision.

Examination tip

Look for clues like 'goaded by what X said' or 'in reaction to what X did'. You will not be expected to reach a firm conclusion because the most difficult issues are for the jury to decide. Remember to explain that there must be a qualifying trigger. State and apply the law and then conclude that "D may be charged with murder, but if the jury are satisfied that a reasonable person would have done the same they can convict of manslaughter".

Remember, there are two things the new law excludes that the old law did not, one under **s 54** and one under **s 55**.

Excluded matters

S 54(4) Revenge: The defence is not allowed if D acted in a 'considered desire for revenge'. It is not clear yet how far this reflects the old law. Revenge is usually carried out after a period of time so would have failed under the sudden and temporary rule in the old law, now it could fail because revenge is excluded by the Act.

S 55 (6) Sexual infidelity: this cannot be a qualifying trigger. Under the old law, it would have been allowed as a cause of the loss of control. However, note that the law was interpreted liberally in **Clinton 2012**, where sexual infidelity was accepted as a 'circumstance' as long as it was integral to the whole situation and not a trigger on its own.

Task 2

Note the point made in each section of the Coroners and Justice Act 2009.

S 54(2)

S 54(4)

S 54(1)(c)

S 54(3)

S 55(6)

Summary of the developments

The characteristics which can be attributed to D to decide if a reasonable person would do as D did have caused some inconsistencies, which have now been clarified to some extent. Age and sex are attributable in all cases. Other characteristics will be part of 'the circumstances of D', so can be taken into account as long as they do not only relate to D's capacity for tolerance or self-restraint. Although not needed for an application of the law, the older cases and the inconsistency will provide material for an evaluation so be aware of the developments and how far these have now been addressed.

DPP v Camplin 1978	only age and sex attributable
Morhall 1993	CA said glue-sniffing was not a characteristic to be attributed to the reasonable person, but this was reversed by HL
Luc Thiet Thuan 1996	mental factors could not be attributed
Smith 2000	everything but excitability, jealousy, obsession and exceptional pugnacity could be attributed
AG v Holley 2005	the jury should not take into account D's mental state, just age and sex, but can then consider how a person would have acted in D's circumstances
S 54 & 55 Coroners and Justice Act 2009	as for Holley, as long as D's circumstances don't relate to the ability to show tolerance or self-restraint
Clinton 2012	sexual infidelity can be a 'circumstance' as long as it is part of the whole

Summary of the provisions under the Coroners' and Justice Act 2009

Did D lose control s 54(1)? However the defence cannot be used where acted in a 'considered desire for revenge' s 54(4)	D must have lost self-control but this need not be sudden s 54(2), however any sign of calming down and/or planning an attack is likely to mean the defence fails
D's act must have resulted from the loss of control s 54(1)(a)	A causation issue, did the loss of control cause D to kill?
There must be a qualifying trigger 55	Did D lose control because of a fear of violence s 55(3)? Did D lose control because of things done or said s 55(4)? Or a combination of these s 55(5)
If the trigger was 'things done or said':- (this is narrower than the old law)	These 'things' must be of an 'extremely grave character' and have caused D to have a justifiable sense of being seriously wronged 55(4)(a) and (b).
Was the trigger excluded by the Act?	If D acted in a considered desire for revenge s 54(4) or the thing 'done or said' constituted sexual infidelity s 55 (6) the defence fails
A person of the same sex and age would have reacted in the same way as D in the same circumstances The jury should ignore matters that affect the ability to retain control.	The old case law is clarified here, i.e., the jury should not take into account mental characteristics which might have made losing control more likely, like a short temper
Did D lose control s 54(1)? However the defence cannot be used where acted in a 'considered desire for revenge' s 54(4)	D must have lost self-control but this need not be sudden s 54(2), however any sign of calming down and/or planning an attack is likely to mean the defence fails

Self-test questions

*To what charge does the **Coroners and Justice Act 2009** apply?*

*What three things need to be proved for **s 54**?*

What amounts to a qualifying trigger?

State two 'characteristics' which are not attributable to the reasonable man.

What 'trigger' is excluded by the Act?

"... a state of mind so different from that of ordinary human beings that the reasonable man would term it abnormal"

Lord Parker

Diminished responsibility comes under the **Homicide Act 1957 s 2(1)** as amended by **s 52** of the **Coroners and Justice Act 2009**. This section came into force in October 2010 and states:

> *"A person who kills or is a party to the killing of another is not to be convicted of murder if he was suffering from an abnormality of mental functioning which:*
>
> *(a) arose from a recognised medical condition,*
>
> *(b) substantially impaired D's ability to:*
>
> *understand the nature of his conduct; or*
>
> *form a rational judgement; or*
>
> *exercise self-control.*
>
> *and*
>
> *(c) provides an explanation for D's acts and omissions in doing or being a party to the killing"*

Examination tip

Note that there is an overlap with loss of control, so you may well have to apply both. Look at the example.

Example

A man's wife is dying and in terrible pain. Over a period of several months, she begs him to end her suffering. He is getting very upset and severely depressed. One night she screams at him "for once in your life act like a man and help me die". He finally snaps and smothers her. This could be 'loss of control' so you would apply the law under **s 54** and **s 55**. There is evidence of loss of self-control, by things 'done or said'. A person with normal levels of tolerance and restraint will be someone who had gone through several months of being tormented by such requests and so arguably would act in the same way. However, if he had spent a couple of days thinking about it, trying to find the courage he may fail on this defence. Under the old law, he would have failed due to the 'sudden and temporary' rule. This no longer applies, but the loss of control defence could still fail if there is a cooling-off period because there may be no loss of control at all. In that case, you can refer to his 'severe depression' and bring in **s 2** as an alternative. In **Bailey 2002**, a 74-year-old man killed his wife, who had motor neurone disease and wanted to die. He had not lost control but his defence of diminished responsibility succeeded.

There are four matters to address under the amended **s 2**

> *D suffers from 'an abnormality of mental functioning'*
>
> *The abnormality arises from a 'recognised medical condition'*
>
> *The abnormality substantially impaired D's ability to do one or more of three specified things*
>
> *The abnormality of mental functioning provides an explanation for D's acts and omissions*

Let's look at each of these.

An abnormality of mental functioning

As this expression indicates, there is an overlap with the general defence of insanity. It covers more than 'defect of reason' though, which is the test for insanity. In **Byrne 1960**, Lord Parker CJ defined abnormality of mind (the old expression) as *"a state of mind so different from that of ordinary human beings that the reasonable man would term it abnormal"*. D was described as a sexual psychopath. While suffering from powerful urges he strangled and then mutilated a young woman. These urges did not prevent him knowing what he was doing (he would have therefore failed on insanity) but he found it difficult, if not impossible, to control them. His defence of diminished responsibility succeeded and he was acquitted of murder.

Cases on the old law will still be relevant in deciding whether there was an abnormality of mental functioning, as the phrase is very similar. It is a matter for the jury based on medical evidence. It is likely that **Byrne** will be followed so that 'abnormality of mental functioning' will be interpreted as a condition which is so different from that of ordinary people that reasonable people (and the jury) would regard it as abnormal.

Arising from a recognised medical condition

In all cases, medical evidence will be needed because the abnormality of mental functioning must arise from a 'recognised medical condition'.

This is perhaps wider than the old law (and a lot less complex) and covers both physical and psychiatric conditions. Disorders such as post-traumatic stress disorder, Gulf War syndrome, paranoid personality disorder, battered woman's syndrome and pre-menstrual stress are all likely to be recognised medical conditions. We looked at **Thornton** with loss of control. She was suffering from 'battered women's syndrome' and at her retrial, the jury accepted the defence of diminished responsibility. In **Martin 2001**, a Norfolk farmer was convicted of murder after killing an intruder. He succeeded in arguing diminished responsibility due to a 'paranoid personality disorder'.

In **Freaney 2011**, a woman was cleared of the murder of her severely autistic 11-year-old son. Her son needed 24-hour care and help with dressing, washing, brushing his teeth and eating. He was not toilet trained and still wore nappies. She murdered him using her coat belt and when she was sure he was dead, she lay down on the bed beside him and tried to commit suicide. She denied murder but admitted his manslaughter on the grounds of diminished responsibility. The jury accepted that she was suffering under 'extreme mental stress' at the time she strangled her son and her plea of diminished responsibility succeeded. She was given a supervision order.

Reference to a recognised medical condition is clearer than the old law, which was complex and hard for juries to understand. However, one problem that remains is one that the Law Commission recognised. They had recommended that developmental immaturity in those under 18 should be included within the definition of diminished responsibility as a recognised medical condition. This was because there is evidence to show that parts of the brain which play an important role in the development of self-control do not mature until 14 years of age. The Government did not act on this suggestion. To an extent it is covered where the lack of maturity is caused by a medical disorder such as autism, but this clearly won't cover all young defendants so a child of 10 or over who kills can be convicted of murder even where there is evidence they had an abnormality of mental functioning due to their undeveloped maturity.

Essay pointer

In **Inglis 2010**, a mother was convicted of murder and sentenced to life imprisonment for killing her disabled son. The facts were similar to **Freaney** and the huge contrast in sentencing in these two cases shows the difficulty in having a mandatory life sentence. Once murder is established the judge

19

has no discretion, so Mrs Inglis was given life even though it was accepted she acted in what she believed were her son's best interests (although this was reduced to a starting point of 9 years rather than the usual 15, on compassionate grounds).

Diminished responsibility and intoxication

Although alcoholism (now usually called alcohol dependency syndrome, or ADS) is a recognised medical condition, intoxication in itself is not. In **Tandy 1989**, an alcoholic strangled her 11-year-old daughter after learning that she had been sexually abused. She had drunk almost a whole bottle of vodka and was suffering from an abnormality of mind at the time of the killing. The CA upheld the conviction for murder and held that the abnormality had to be caused by the disease of alcoholism rather than by the voluntary taking of alcohol. It could succeed if the first drink was involuntary but on the evidence, this was not the case. The CA established the principle that drink is only capable of giving rise to this defence if it either causes brain damage or produces an irresistible craving so that consumption is involuntary (ADS).

So an abnormality caused by taking drugs or drink would not suffice unless there is an associated medical condition. However, if D is intoxicated *as well as* suffering from one of the above causes the defence may succeed. This was stated in **Fenton 1975**, confirmed in **Gittens 1984** (where she was drunk but also suffered from chronic depression) and approved by the HL in **Dietschmann 2003**. It is thus a well-established rule which will still apply under the new law.

Key case

In **Dietschmann**, D had savagely attacked someone whilst suffering depression following the death of his girlfriend. He was also drunk. The HL made clear that D had to show that even without the drink he had sufficient 'abnormality of mind' (as in **Fenton** and **Gittens**). However, they added that he did not have to show that he would have killed even if not intoxicated, because the 'abnormality' did not have to be the *only* cause of the killing. This means D only needs to satisfy the jury that, as well as (but not *because of*) being drunk, he had an abnormality which substantially impaired his responsibility. He need not show he would still have killed even if he had been sober. The HL held that the jury must ask themselves whether D had satisfied them that, *despite the drink*, his mental abnormality substantially impaired his responsibility. If so, the defence may succeed, if not, the defence is not available.

Essay pointer

These are difficult issues, not least if you happen to be on the jury! You will have to try to ignore the intoxication and determine whether the other causes were enough substantially to impair D's ability. This is not an easy task. The **Dietschmann** case highlights the difficulties. Does it solve any? Would you be able ignore the intoxication in such cases if you were on the jury?

If alcoholism as a disease is argued, the jury will have to decide if the first drink taken was voluntary or involuntary.

The rules were clarified in the next case.

In **Wood 2008**, the CA confirmed that **Dietschmann** did not alter the principle that voluntary consumption of alcohol does not amount to an abnormality of the mind, but said that it did establish that a defence of diminished responsibility would not fail merely because D had consumed alcohol voluntarily before killing. The CA agreed that **Tandy** should be re-assessed in cases where there was 'alcohol dependency syndrome'. In **Wood**, D had been diagnosed with this syndrome and killed in a frenzied attack whilst drunk, having woken after a party to find a man attempting to have oral sex with him. The CA held that it was not a requirement that the syndrome caused brain damage (as required in **Tandy**). The only question for the jury was whether it constituted an abnormality of mind (now mental functioning). If it did not, diminished responsibility based on the consumption of alcohol would fail. If it did, the jury must consider whether D's responsibility was substantially impaired because of the syndrome. The jury should focus exclusively on the effect of alcohol consumed as a direct result of the illness or disease and ignore the effect of any alcohol consumed voluntarily.

In **Dowds 2012**, in an appeal to the CA after the **2009 Act** came into force, D argued that acute intoxication was a recognised medical condition. He and his partner had a long history of drunkenness and violence, and both had been drinking when he attacked her with a knife and killed her. His appeal failed and the CA held that the new law was not intended to change the rule that voluntary intoxication was not capable of establishing diminished responsibility.

These are difficult issues so let's sum up the recent cases.

> *If D has a medical condition and is also drunk, the jury should ignore the drink and just consider the medical condition (Dietschmann).*

> *If the intoxication results from a medical condition, such as alcohol dependency syndrome, the jury can consider the drink but must ask whether it amounts to an abnormality (Wood).*

> *The Coroners and Justice Act 2009 does not change the rules on this (Dowds).*

Example

After Tony came back from fighting in the war in Iraq he was diagnosed with post-traumatic stress disorder (PTSD), which causes him to have violent outbursts. One night, after several drinks, he gets into a fight and kills someone. He is charged with murder and pleads the defence of diminished responsibility. The PTSD will be a recognised medical condition, so the jury will then have to decide whether the PTSD itself substantially impaired his ability to exercise self-control, ignoring the effect of the drinks he had consumed.

Substantially impaired D's ability

'Substantially impaired' will be interpreted in the way same as the old law. The judge will usually direct the jury as to the meaning of 'substantial' in relation to the facts of the case. In **Lloyd 1967**, the court said the impairment need not be total but must be more than trivial or minimal. In **Campbell 1987**, the medical evidence was that D had epilepsy which could make him "vulnerable to an impulsive tendency". The defence failed because 'vulnerable to' indicates that it was not substantial.

There is some difference with the previous law. Under **s 2** as amended by the **Coroners and Justice Act**, it is not D's mental responsibility that must be substantially impaired, it is D's ability to do one of three things:

> *to understand the nature of his conduct, or*

> *to form a rational judgement or,*

> *to exercise self-control*

Although not specified in the old law, these matters are much as before. Someone with learning difficulties may not understand the nature of the act, nor be able to form a rational judgement, nor exercise self-control. **Byrne** succeeded because he was unable to exercise self-control and this is likely to be the same now. Severe stress, as in many of the mercy killing cases, would perhaps prevent D being able to form a rational judgement.

Note that only one of the three things is needed, not all.

In **Zebedee 2011** (unreported), D had killed his father who was suffering from Alzheimer's disease. He admitted killing him but denied murder. He said that he snapped after remembering alleged abuse by his father that he had suffered as a child, but there was no evidence to support this. He argued both diminished responsibility and loss of control, saying that his ability to exercise control had been impaired by an adjustment order resulting from the earlier abuse. As for loss of control, he said this was caused by his father repeatedly whistling a tune, soiling himself and making a gesture which recalled the abuse. Both defences were put to the jury but rejected.

Provides an explanation for D's acts and omissions in doing or being a party to the killing.

That the abnormality of mental functioning must 'provide an explanation for D's acts and omissions' is clarified in **s 52(1)(c)** of the Act as meaning that it 'causes, or is a significant contributory factor in causing, D to carry out that conduct'.

This was introduced to the defence by the amendments made by the **Coroners and Justice Act 2009**. It means that there must now be some causal connection between D's abnormality of mental functioning and the conduct. The abnormality must cause the killing or make a significant contribution to it.

Example: Applying the 2009 Act to Wood, above.

Alcohol dependency syndrome was confirmed to be a recognised medical condition in this case.

The jury would also need to be convinced that:

D was suffering an abnormality of mental functioning which arose from his alcohol dependency syndrome

This abnormality substantially (not trivially, but not necessarily totally, using **Lloyd**) impaired his ability to do one of the following:

> understand the nature of his conduct: quite likely, the evidence showed he did not know what he was doing at the time
>
> form a rational judgement: also likely as it was doubtful he could form any judgement at all
>
> exercise self-control: not clear on the facts but we only need one of these not all three

Finally, the abnormality of mental functioning must provide an explanation for his acts. An issue of causation, and again quite likely as he would not have killed if not suffering from the syndrome, so this made a significant contribution to his actions.

Task 3

Go to the Law Commission website and look at the 2004 report on 'Partial defences to murder' or the 2006 report on 'Murder, manslaughter and infanticide' (listed in the A-Z). Quotes and discussions from these will enhance an essay and help you see how far the **Coroners and Justice Act** took up the LC's suggestions.

Burden of proof

Unlike loss of control, where the prosecution has to show that D was *not* provoked, D must prove diminished responsibility. The standard of proof is the balance of probabilities, i.e., the civil standard. Remember: D will need to provide medical evidence to support the plea of diminished responsibility.

Essay pointer

There may be a sense of injustice where a jury decision is based on what is felt to be acceptable rather than by applying the legal tests to the facts. The defence may succeed or fail for moral reasons, rather than legal ones.

Examples can be seen in cases of 'mercy killings', such as **Freany** and **Bailey** above. A jury may accept a plea of diminished responsibility even where there is little evidence for it. This may be due to sympathy for the accused, or because the mandatory life sentence means that if the defence fails, the sentence will be life for murder. Accepting the defence means that a discretionary sentence can be given, taking into account the circumstances. Whilst this may 'do justice' in a particular case, it is arguably stretching the law to fit the prevailing moral standards of the jury.

It also works both ways. In **Sutcliffe 1981**, the 'Yorkshire ripper' case where D had committed a series of brutal murders, the defence was rejected by the jury despite strong medical evidence to support it, and the fact that both the defence and prosecution accepted it. Presumably, the brutality of the murders persuaded the jury that a life sentence was appropriate.

Abolishing the mandatory life sentence for murder could be discussed in an evaluation. It would perhaps avoid the uncertainty of relying on the jury's sympathy or revulsion.

Examination tip

Remember that there is an overlap between loss of control and diminished responsibility. Look back at cases like **Thornton**. Long-term abuse may be relevant to loss of control or result in a recognised medical condition such as 'battered woman's syndrome' or trauma. You may well have to discuss both defences. Look carefully at the given facts and watch for words like 'abuse' or 'depression'.

Summary

Abnormality of mental functioning: will be interpreted as for abnormality of mind ...	... so different from that of ordinary human beings that the reasonable man would term it abnormal **Byrne 1960**
Substantially impaired	Impairment need not be total but must be more than trivial or minimal **Lloyd 1967**
It is D's ability to do one of three things which must be substantially impaired	These are: to understand the nature of his conduct; to form a rational judgement; to exercise self-control.
Alcoholism, or alcohol dependency syndrome, may lead to a successful defence but only if the first drink was involuntary	**Tandy 1989/Wood 2008**
If D is intoxicated *as well as* suffering from a abnormality of mental functioning the defence may succeed, but the jury must ignore the intoxication	**Dietschmann 2003**
The **Coroners and Justice Act 2009** does not change the rules on intoxication	**Dowds 2012**
The abnormality of mental functioning must provide an explanation for D's conduct	A causation issue; did the abnormality of mental functioning cause D to act that way?

Problems and reforms

In their 2004 report 'Partial Defences to Murder', the Law Commission said

> *"Over the centuries the law of homicide, including the law of murder, has developed in a higgledy-piggledy fashion. The present law is a product of judge made law supplemented by Parliament's sporadic intervention. The outcome is a body of law characterised by a lack of clarity and coherence."*

In their 2006 report 'Murder, manslaughter and Infanticide' the Law Commission said that the two-category structure of murder or manslaughter is out-dated. The LC felt someone who killed, e.g., under provocation should still be called a murderer but should not have a life sentence. They recommended a three-tier structure for homicide, which would cover

1st-degree murder

2nd-degree murder (

Manslaughter

Only the first of these would have a mandatory life sentence and voluntary manslaughter using the partial defences would come under 2nd degree murder.

The LC also wanted a new **Homicide Act** to provide clear and comprehensive definitions of the homicide offences and the partial defences.

These recommendations have not been taken up and the **Coroners and Justice Act** only addresses a few of the problems highlighted in their reports.

Key criticisms of the special defences

The defence of provocation, now loss of control, has been improved by the Coroners and Justice Act, although some argue that it is still unclear. One improvement is that reacting in fear of serious violence is a stated to be qualifying trigger, thus clarifying this somewhat

The removal of the need for a 'sudden and temporary' loss of control is an improvement. However, the fact that any loss of control must be shown goes against the Law Commission's proposals and prevents the defence clearly extending to cases of abuse against women, who may be physically weaker and liable to even greater abuse if they lose control and fight back

The 'fear of serious violence' trigger addresses the 'all-or-nothing' nature of self-defence. If excessive force is used, there may now be a defence of loss of control

Diminished responsibility is not a satisfactory alternative for abused women as it indicates they are mentally unbalanced

Where there is evidence of intoxication as well as another cause of 'abnormality' the jury has to perform an almost impossible task of separating the one from the other – Dietschmann

'Abnormality of mental functioning' is difficult for the jury to understand and medical evidence is often complex and contradictory

Diminished responsibility is sometimes dependent on whether the killing was morally wrong – Bailey/Sutcliffe

Success may depend on which defence is raised in the first place. What was then provocation failed in the case of Cocker 1989, but diminished responsibility succeeded in Bailey 2002 in similar circumstances. Provocation failed in Thornton, but at her retrial diminished responsibility succeeded, suggesting that this defence should have been raised at her original trial

Unlike most defences, for diminished responsibility the burden of proof is on D

There is an overlap between diminished responsibility and loss of control where the killing has been due to a mental state such as depression or long-term abuse (Aluwahlia and Thornton)

The difficulties of these defences for the jury could lead to inconsistency. Juries may differ in their decisions because of a different understanding of the facts and of how the defences should apply

Should the mandatory life sentence for murder be abolished? If it was, then it could be argued that these defences would not be necessary. On the other hand, abolishing them and leaving the issue as one of sentencing would remove the role of the jury. It is arguably better for a jury to decide, for example, how a 'reasonable person' would act

Should the LC's recommendations of a three-tiered system have been taken up? If it was, then again it could be argued that these defences would not be necessary

Self-test questions

From which case did the opening quote come?

What type of evidence will be required for this defence?

Who has the burden of proving the defence?

*Which Act amends the **Homicide Act s 2** on the defence of diminished responsibility?*

Revision

A general guide to revision

The first and foremost rule for revision is to start early. Too many students leave it until the last minute and then get in a panic. If you take it gently and organise your time properly you will feel a lot more calm and confident when exam time comes. Make a plan of what you want to cover each day and try to stick to it. Don't forget to include some breaks in your schedule, if you are tired it will be harder to retain the material you have been revising.

Here are a few tips for revision techniques

Go through your notes and try to summarise them

Learn the key cases, as these are essential to know

Make sure you understand how the judge has applied the law to the facts so you can do the same in an examination scenario

If the case is one you may also want to use in an essay, be sure you understand any problems it raises or solves and / or the concept of law that is involved

Example

In **Brown**, the judges decided that consent was not a defence to serious harm, so this would apply to a scenario involving GBH.

It raises a problem in the law, because the reasoning was obscure. It was not sufficiently clear why the consent defence failed. It could be argued that the defence fails if harm was intended (this would apply to s 18 but not 20), or alternatively that the defence fails if harm was serious (this would apply to both s 18 and 20).

Another problem, and one which relates to the concept of law and morals, is that some of the judges seemed to rely on their own moral values when reaching their decision.

Go through the summaries of the topic, these provide a base of the essential points which may need to be addressed

Go to the examination board's website for past exam papers, mark schemes and reports

Practice answering questions then look at the examiners' mark schemes and reports to see if you were on the right track

Revision of voluntary manslaughter

The first thing to remember is that the special defences only apply where there is a charge of murder, so revise *actus reus*, *mens rea* and murder carefully.

Examination tip: problem questions

In a problem question, look out for anything that D can argue broke the chain of causation. For example, D attacks someone who is hit by a car or bus when running away from the attack. **Roberts** can be used to say that this is unlikely to break the chain. Look out for words like 'near the road' or 'in the bus station'. These suggest it is foreseeable and if serious harm was intended in the original attack, it could be murder. If V refuses treatment, you may need the 'thin-skull' rule. Here look out for the reason. If it is a completely idiotic decision, then **Blaue** may be distinguished. If it is due to religious beliefs, it will be followed. If the chain of causation is broken then there is no *actus reus* of murder so it cannot be voluntary manslaughter either.

Murder, the killing of a human being with intent to kill or seriously injure, is probably the most socially unacceptable crime. It carries a mandatory life sentence, which means the judge has no discretion when passing sentence.

The two defences which are specific to murder, if successful, reduce murder to manslaughter, and thus allow sentencing to be at the discretion of the judge. It is called voluntary manslaughter, because D admits killing but argues that there were special circumstances which mean the conviction should be for manslaughter not murder. These circumstances are loss of control (D killed in reaction to something done or said by the victim) or diminished responsibility (D was suffering from some kind of mental abnormality).

> *They are called special defences because they only apply to the specific crime of murder, unlike the other general defences*

> *They are called partial defences because they only partially excuse the behaviour, there is still a conviction but for manslaughter, not murder*

Murder, somewhat surprisingly, is not a statutory offence. It comes from the common law not an Act of Parliament. Murder and voluntary manslaughter have the same *actus reus* and *mens rea*. The difference lies in these defences.

Example

Jane picks up a knife and stabs Jenny, who dies. Jane has the *actus reus* of murder as her act has caused Jenny's death. She also has the *mens rea* because she intended to kill, or at least seriously harm, her. Jane will be sentenced to life imprisonment.

If Jenny had taunted Jane in some way, Jane may be able to use the defence of loss of control if this is what caused her to stab Jenny. If she is suffering from some kind of mental disability at the time, Jane may argue diminished responsibility. If either defence succeeds, Jane will be convicted of manslaughter, not murder. The judge can choose the sentence.

Examination tip: evaluation questions

All the matters in the essay pointers discussions are ones which can be used in an evaluation essay, using the cases to illustrate what you say. There are usually valid arguments on both sides so don't attempt to write what you think examiners want to see; an examiner will be much more impressed with a balanced argument. It is acceptable to have an opinion, but look at the issue from the other point of view too; this shows you have considered the arguments before reaching your own (balanced) opinion.

Examination tip: general

Make sure that in an examination question you cover murder before moving on to the defences. Be selective and keep it relevant. You may only need to discuss murder briefly, especially if both intent and causation are clear. Look for clues to see which defence is most appropriate, e.g., if there is evidence of depression or some kind of trauma it is likely to be diminished responsibility. If there is something which triggered D's reaction (fear of violence or something 'done or said') then loss of control should be discussed. You may need both, so read back over the defences to ensure you can see the overlap.

Loss of control

Under **s 54**, of the **Coroners and Justice Act 2009** there are three questions to consider:

did D lose self-control?

was the loss of self-control triggered by something specified in s 55?

would a normal person of D's sex and age have reacted in the same way in D's circumstances?

Under **S 55(1)** the loss of control must be triggered by:

D's fear of serious violence from V against D or another identified person; or

a thing or things done or said (or both) which:

(a) constituted circumstances of an extremely grave character, and

(b) caused D to have a justifiable sense of being seriously wronged

Excluded matters

S 54(4) revenge and **s 55 (6)** sexual infidelity (but note that the latter may be included in 'D's **circumstances'** see **Clinton 2012**)

Diminished responsibility

Under **s 2** of the **Homicide Act** as amended by the **Coroners and Justice Act 2009** there must be

an abnormality of mental functioning

which arises from a 'recognised medical condition'

and substantially impaired D's ability to do one or more of three specified things

and provides an explanation for D's acts and omissions

The specified things are:

to understand the nature of his conduct, or

to form a rational judgement or,

to exercise self-control

Task 4

As well as any recent cases, older ones will still be needed for interpreting the **Coroners and Justice Act** where relevant. From which cases did the following principles come?

That sexual infidelity may be relevant to the circumstances of D, even though excluded by s 55

That an 'abnormality of mind' (now mental functioning) for diminished responsibility is one that reasonable people would term abnormal

That an abnormality caused by alcoholism may be accepted as diminished responsibility

That impairment of responsibility need not be total but must be more than trivial

That where there is evidence of intoxication as well as another cause of 'abnormality' the jury should ignore the intoxication

Task 5

Make a separate folder for the more detailed material you need for essays. As you read cases start to question what is satisfactory – or not – about the law and add your thoughts to the folder. Look out for articles from newspapers or law journals on any of the issues you are discussing. Cut them out and put them in the folder, adding a few of your own comments. Keep this folder for revision.

Task 6 Loss of control

The new defence of loss of control has three main elements:

(a) the defendant's conduct resulted from a loss of self-control;

(b) the loss of self-control had a qualifying trigger;

(c) a person of the defendant's sex and age with an ordinary level of tolerance and self-restraint and in the circumstances of the defendant might have acted in the same or similar way to the defendant.

Copy the diagram and complete the two columns on the right to compare the new law with the old.

Old law	New law	Case (where appropriate)
Homicide Act s 3		
Defence called provocation		
There must be a sudden loss of control		
Would a reasonable person do as D did in the circumstances?		
No qualifying trigger		
Nothing specifically excluded		

Task 7 Case study on diminished responsibility

Read the case and then answer the questions. You can use old cases in support of application of the law in this area, as appropriate.

In **Wood 2008**, D had been drinking heavily and fell asleep in the victim's flat. When he awoke, he found the victim sexually abusing him and hit him repeatedly with a meat clever. V died and D was charged with murder. He was convicted and appealed on the basis that he had 'alcohol dependency syndrome'. The CA confirmed that **Dietschmann** did nothing to alter the principle that voluntary consumption of alcohol did not amount to an abnormality of the mind, but said that it did establish that a defence of diminished responsibility would not fail merely because D had consumed alcohol voluntarily before killing. The CA held that **Dietschmann** had diluted the principles in **Tandy**. Disapproving **Tandy** the CA held that in cases where there was 'alcohol dependency syndrome' the principles needed to be reassessed. If there was brain damage this may help to persuade the jury that the defendant suffered from an 'abnormality of mind induced by disease or illness' but it did not need to be proved that the syndrome had caused brain damage. The only question for the jury was whether D's syndrome constituted an abnormality of mind. If it did not constitute such an abnormality of mind, diminished responsibility based on the consumption of alcohol would fail. If it did, the jury must consider whether D's mental responsibility was substantially impaired as a result of the syndrome. In doing so, the jury should focus exclusively on the effect of alcohol consumed as a direct result of the illness or disease and ignore the effect of any alcohol consumed voluntarily.

What would be substituted for the phrase 'abnormality of the mind' under the new law?

Under what Act of Parliament is the new law found?

What was the principle in Tandy?

What was the principle in Dietschmann?

How do you think the law on diminished responsibility and intoxication will apply to the Wood case now?

Can you see a problem with the law as interpreted in Wood?

Examination practice

Although different exam boards have different ways of styling their examination papers, there are always going to be common elements. You will need to be able to apply the law you have learnt to a particular scenario and you will need to be able to evaluate a given topic to provide a critique of the law, including reforms where appropriate.

A general guide to examination papers

Read **all** questions carefully before deciding which to answer

Look again at the ones you wish to answer to make sure you can do so, make brief notes - this can be a useful checklist later when you are tired and your memory begins to fail.

Structure your answer. Remember this is a test of law so you need to state the legal principles involved and apply them to the particular question. A solid start is worth a lot and gets the examiner on your side. A small plan is helpful.

It is necessary to do more than regurgitate your notes. You need to be selective as to what is relevant, and to choose appropriate cases and examples in support of what you say.

Never put in irrelevant material just because you know it - there is **never** a question asking you to 'write all you know about...'. The examiner wants to know that you understand the specific issues and can apply the appropriate law to the facts given.

Always support your answer with **relevant** cases. Don't worry too much about the facts, the principle forming the *ratio decidendi* is usually the important part e.g. in **Donoghue v Stevenson** that you owe a duty to others to take care is vital but you don't need to write a paragraph discussing snails and ginger beer

Having said that, you want to show why you have chosen a particular case so will need to mention any facts that specifically relate to the scenario. If the scenario mentions someone being ill after consuming a chocolate bar with a dead mouse in it (yes, there has been a case!) then talking briefly about snails in ginger beer will be relevant. The main point here is that you need to be selective; this demonstrates a skill in itself and conserves precious time.

If you can't remember the name of a case that is relevant, don't leave it out but refer to it in a general way e.g. 'in one decided case....' or 'in a similar case....'

In problem questions, identify the various issues in the first paragraph and then set about dealing with them one by one, applying the relevant law and cases to each issue, **referring to the facts of the question as you do so**. This tells the examiner that you are answering the specific points raised. A short summing up is also a good idea e.g., "In conclusion it would appear that D may be liable for ... but it is possible that the defence of ... applies which will reduce/negate liability"

In essay questions, you will usually be asked to form an opinion or to weigh up arguments for and against a particular statement. Here a broader range of knowledge is needed showing arguments for, arguments against and an evaluation of these arguments. If reforms have been proposed or implemented, discuss these too. You should always round off your answer with a short concluding paragraph, preferably using some of the wording from the question to indicate to the examiner that you are addressing the specific issue raised.

Essays should have a logical structure. The beginning, should introduce the subject matter, the central part should explain/analyse/criticise it as appropriate, and the conclusion should bring the various strands of argument together with reference to the question set.

Try to consider alternative arguments. A well-rounded essay will bring in other views even if you disagree with them; you cannot shoot them down without setting them up first.

Writing a discussion essay: staging the information logically.

If you stage your essay as follows, it will make it easy to read, logically structured and easier to write. It may also mean you don't leave out important points. Here's how it works:

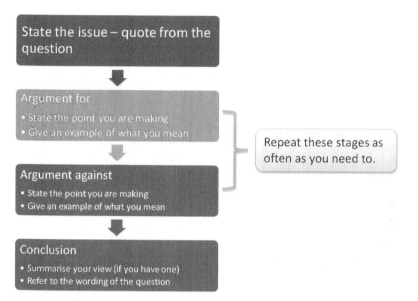

Writing each paragraph: making each one logical and easy to read (and write!).

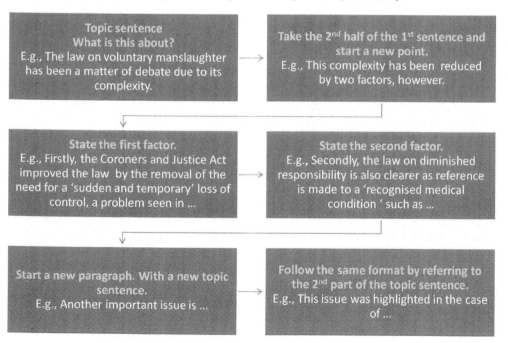

Finally, make sure you cover the whole question. For both problem and evaluation questions, there are only a certain number of marks available. The examiner has a mark scheme to work to, so however brilliant your answer to one part of the question is, missing out the other parts will severely reduce your total marks.

Examination practice for voluntary manslaughter

Problem scenarios (application)

The special defences only apply to murder so this needs to be proved first. The law on AR and MR prepares you for answering problem questions on murder and voluntary manslaughter (which have the same AR and MR remember). Murder can be committed by an omission (**Gibbins & Proctor**), it is a result crime so it must be proved that D's act caused death factually (**White**) and in law (**Cheshire/Roberts**). Murder requires the MR of intent (**Nedrick/Woollin**) to kill or seriously injure (**Smith**).

Examination tip

In all problem questions, you need to take a logical approach. First, read the facts carefully to ensure that you understand the points raised by the scenario. Then apply the relevant law in a logical manner, using cases in support. A sound application of the law requires you to be selective. The facts should point you to particular issues which need addressing and you must be prepared to pick out the relevant law and cases and to leave out anything irrelevant – for which you will gain no marks.

Examples

Matt has just come back from serving with the army in Afghanistan and is suffering from post-traumatic stress disorder (PTSD). He thinks his neighbour Mike is an enemy spy and shoots him. Matt has both the *actus reus* and *mens rea* of murder so this can be dealt with very briefly. You will need to discuss the **Homicide Act** (as amended by the **Coroners and Justice Act**) defence of diminished responsibility in detail to decide whether he can use this defence to reduce the conviction to manslaughter. PTSD is a recognised medical condition so the focus is on whether this caused an abnormality of mental functioning and if so whether it substantially impaired his ability to do one of the three specified things, e.g., to form a rational judgement.

Matt has just come back from serving with the army in Afghanistan. He gets into a fight with his neighbour Mike who calls him a coward. Matt is very upset as he fought bravely and often risked his life, so he pulls out a knife and kills Mike. Use of the knife shows intent to seriously injure even if he did not intend to kill so again, Matt has the *actus reus* and *mens rea* of murder and this can be dealt with very briefly. The main issue here is loss of control so you would need to discuss the **Coroners and Justice Act** defence, in particular whether there was a qualifying trigger. This can be 'things said' so the question is whether what Mike said constituted matters of an 'extremely grave' character and whether this caused Matt to have 'a justifiable sense of being seriously wronged'.

Examination tip

It is **good practice** to select only the law that applies to the given facts. This shows that you understand the law well enough to know what is relevant.

It is **bad practice** to write all you know about an area just because you know it well. Even if it is right, you will gain no marks if it is not relevant to the facts given

All exam questions can be approached in a similar way:

identify the law

state the law (using relevant cases)

apply the law (using relevant cases)

reach a conclusion (based on your application)

Task 8 Application practice: Loss of control

Look up the facts of the following cases and consider what caused D to lose control and kill (what 'triggered' the action). Then apply the new law to see if the conclusion would be the same now.

Doughty

Thornton

Ahluwalia

Baillie

Task 9 Application practice: Diminished responsibility

In **Freaney 2011**, a woman was charged with the murder of her severely autistic 11-year-old son. Mrs Freaney denied murder but admitted manslaughter on the grounds of diminished responsibility due to the severe stress she was suffering. Her son needed 24-hour care and help with dressing, washing, brushing his teeth and eating. He was not toilet trained and still wore nappies. She killed her son using her coat belt and when she was sure he was dead she lay down on the bed beside him and tried to commit suicide.

Apply the law to these facts to decide whether she was guilty of murder or manslaughter.

Task 10 Clue spotting – application practice

There is limited time in most exams and examiners rarely set a question which requires you to cover everything. To practise being selective do the following exercise.

The scenario shows that someone has died following an intentional act by D. Look at the brief comments taken from the scenarios and consider what they indicate is the focus of the question, with a case if appropriate. The first one is done for you as an example.

Phrase from scenario	Focus
Angry at what he said D ...	Loss of control, specifically that it can be triggered by 'things done or said' (Doughty)
D thought over what had been said and got very angry, the next day he ...	
D had been suffering from severe depression and ...	
D was suffering from severe depression and after several drinks he ...	
D had suffered years of abuse and one day just 'lost it' and ...	

Essay questions (evaluation)

The 'Essay pointers' and 'Key criticisms' are intended to provide you with information to use in an essay where you have to evaluate a given area of law. Look through these before doing the evaluation practice below.

This is an example of a typical exam question

'Despite some reforms, there are still criticisms to be made regarding the current law of voluntary manslaughter. Discuss how far the law is still unsatisfactory and whether any further reforms are needed'.

Again, a logical approach is needed. You should:

State what the current law is

Discuss where it remains unsatisfactory

Support your comments with cases and/or examples

Discuss whether and where reforms are still needed

The following exercise will give you a basis for such a discussion.

Task 11 Evaluation practice

Look at the brief comments below and then:

State what the current law is, using cases where appropriate

Expand on the statement (this can be for or against it or just a brief comment of your own)

Support your comments with cases and/or examples

If reforms have been implemented or proposed, add these

There is no 'right' answer to evaluation questions, opinions vary and you can form your own – but **always** use cases and/or examples to back up what you say.

The removal of the need for a 'sudden and temporary' loss of control is an improvement

The Coroners and Justice Act has improved the law as the defence of loss of control is now much wider than under the Homicide Act

There is no need for women to rely on loss of control as long-term abuse has been recognised as a medical condition

Reacting in fear of serious violence is stated to be qualifying trigger, thus clarifying the law somewhat

The new law on diminished responsibility is much clearer, especially as regards medical evidence

Abolishing the mandatory life sentence for murder would remove the need for the special defences

Answers to tasks and self-test questions

Task 1

This task just requires you to make some notes. Keep these for revision.

Task 2

> **S 54(2) The loss of self-control does not need to be sudden**
>
> **S 54(4) The defence is not allowed if D acted in a 'considered desire for revenge'**
>
> **S 54(1)(c) A person of D's age or sex would have reacted in the same way**
>
> **S 54(3) Reference can be made to all D's circumstances other than those whose only relevance to D's conduct is that they bear on D's general capacity for tolerance or self-restraint**
>
> **S 55(6) If the thing 'done or said' constituted sexual infidelity it is to be disregarded. Also excluded is where D has incited either the fear of violence or the thing done or said, in order to have the excuse to use violence**

Self-test questions Chapter 2

> The **Coroners and Justice Act 2009** applies to murder
>
> The three things which need to be proved for **s 54** are
>
> > that D lost self-control
> >
> > the loss of self-control was triggered by something specified in **s 55**
> >
> > a normal person of D's sex and age would have reacted in the same way in D's circumstances
>
> The qualifying triggers are
>
> > D's fear of serious violence from V against D or another identified person; or
> >
> > a thing or things done or said (or both) which –
> >
> > (a) constituted circumstances of an extremely grave character, and
> >
> > (b) caused D to have a justifiable sense of being seriously wronged
> >
> > or a combination of both of these
>
> Two 'characteristics' which are not attributable to the reasonable man are jealousy and obsession.
>
> The Act specifically excludes sexual infidelity as a qualifying trigger.

Task 3

As for Task 1 above, this required you to make some notes for later revision. Both reports apply to an evaluation of murder and the 2004 one specifically applies to the partial defences which make it voluntary manslaughter

Self-test questions Chapter 3

> The opening quote came from **Byrne 1960**.

*Medical evidence will be required for a **s 2** defence.*

The defendant has the burden of proving the defence.

*The **Coroners and Justice Act 2009** amended the **Homicide Act s 2** on the defence of diminished responsibility.*

Task 4

The appropriate cases are added following the principles

Sexual infidelity may be relevant to the circumstances of D, even though excluded by s 55 – Clinton 2012

An 'abnormality of mind' (now mental functioning) for diminished responsibility is one that reasonable people would term abnormal – Byrne 1960

An abnormality caused by alcoholism may be accepted as diminished responsibility – Tandy 1989

Impairment of responsibility need not be total but must be more than trivial – Lloyd 1967

Where there is evidence of intoxication as well as another cause of 'abnormality' the jury should ignore the intoxication – Dietschmann 2003.

Task 5

This task just requires you to make some notes. Keep these for revision

Task 6 Loss of control

Old law	New law	Case (where appropriate)
Homicide Act s 3	Coroners and Justice Act 2009 s 54 & 55	-
Defence called provocation	Defence called loss of control	-
There must be a sudden loss of control	There must be a loss of control	**Ahluwalia/Thornton** could succeed now but only if there is a loss of control
Would a reasonable person do as D did in the circumstances?	Would a person of D's sex and age, with a normal degree of tolerance and self-restraint and in the circumstances of D, have reacted in the same way as D?	**Camplin** and **Holley** still apply but not Smith. It is now clearer that only sex and age are relevant to how someone in D's position would act
No qualifying trigger	The qualifying triggers are • fear of serious violence or • thing(s) done and/or said which not only constituted circumstances of an extremely grave character but also caused D to have a justifiable sense of being seriously wronged; or • a combination of these	**Ahluwalia/Thornton** could succeed as there was fear of serious violence, but there must be a loss of control Doughty could fail now
Nothing specifically excluded	Two things are excluded, revenge and sexual infidelity	**Clinton 2012** indicates that sexual infidelity can be included as a circumstance (but not as the sole trigger)

Task 7 Case study on diminished responsibility

The phrase abnormality of mental functioning would be substituted for 'abnormality of the mind' under the new law.

The new law is found under the **Coroners and Justice Act 2009 s 52**.

The principle in **Tandy** was that the abnormality had to be caused by the disease of alcoholism rather than by the voluntary taking of alcohol. Drink is only capable of giving rise to a defence if it either causes brain damage or produces an irresistible craving so that consumption is involuntary (but on the evidence in **Tandy** this was not the case).

The principle in **Dietschmann** was that the 'abnormality' did not have to be the *only* cause of the killing. If D is intoxicated as well as suffering from an abnormality, the defence may succeed and D does not have to show that he would have killed even if not intoxicated.

Alcohol dependency syndrome would be a recognised medical condition; it was questionable whether the abnormality of mental functioning arose from this, however. The CA thought it could have and quashed the conviction. According to **Dietschmann**, D need not show that he would have killed even if sober; the intoxication can be ignored by the jury as long as there is *also* an abnormality of mental functioning. If the abnormality arose from a recognised condition (the alcohol dependency syndrome) then Wood would probably succeed in the defence, as it seems to have substantially impaired his ability to do one of the three specified things, in particular to control himself.

One problem with the law as interpreted in **Wood** is whether it is realistic to expect the jury to ignore the effect of the intoxication on D. Can a person really do this when deciding whether D's mental abnormality substantially impaired his ability to, e.g., exercise control? It can be said that **Tandy** was too strict in not allowing her drinking to support the defence when she was clearly unable to control it. As the law is now interpreted, if the 'alcohol dependency syndrome' did not constitute an abnormality of mental functioning, diminished responsibility based on the consumption of alcohol would fail. If it did constitute an abnormality of mental functioning, the jury must go on to consider whether D's ability was substantially impaired as a result of the syndrome. The CA said the jury should focus only on the effect of alcohol consumed as a direct result of the illness or disease and ignore the effect of any voluntary drinking. This still seems quite a difficult task.

Task 8 Application practice: loss of control

Doughty

D lost control because of 'things done or said' – the baby's crying. This caused D's act. Under the new law it would be very unlikely to be a 'qualifying trigger' however, as **s 55** states that the 'things done or said' must constitute circumstances of an extremely grave character, and cause D to have a justifiable sense of being seriously wronged. A crying baby is not likely to be seen as either of these things, and it is probable that the defence would fail now.

NB It is possible it would have failed before, the appeal succeeded because the matter was never allowed to go before a jury

Thornton

Years of abuse by her husband was the trigger. This would be specifically within **s 55** of the new Act which refers to 'fear of serious violence' as a qualifying trigger. Her only problem may be convincing the jury that she lost control in the first place. If the prosecution can show that she did not lose control, the defence would still fail. The fact that she went to the kitchen to calm down may convince the jury that she was in control of herself at the time she acted, so the killing did not result from a loss of control as required by **s 54**.

Ahluwalia

Again, the trigger was years of abuse by her husband. This would be specifically within **s 55** of the new Act which refers to 'fear of serious violence' as a qualifying trigger. As with **Thornton**, she may have a problem convincing the jury that she lost control in the first place. If the prosecution can show she did not lose control the defence would still fail. The fact that she waited until her husband was asleep may again persuade the jury that her actions were not caused by the loss of control. It may even mean the judge does not put the matter before the jury at all, as there must be some evidence she actually lost control and waiting until he was asleep makes this unlikely.

Baillie

The threat to his son may be enough to qualify as a trigger for his loss of control because **s 55** says the fear of violence from V may be 'against D or another identified person'. The threat to his son may therefore suffice. The problem for Baillie may lie in the fact that there is an element of revenge in his act, (you threatened my son, so I'll hurt you). This is one of the matters specifically excluded in **s 54(2)** of the **Coroners and Justice Act 2009**. This case could go either way now. It may fail on loss of control itself, depending on how long a time elapsed between the loss of control at hearing of the threat and the killing. There is no longer a need for a 'sudden and temporary' loss of control, but **s 54** requires that the killing 'resulted' from the loss of control, so any time lapse may convince a jury that the killing was not caused by the loss of control. If he lost control and went immediately to the dealer's house he may succeed; much will depend on the length of any time lapse.

*NB As with **Doughty**, D's appeal succeeded because the matter was not put to the jury. The jury may well have decided he had not killed due to a loss of control – especially as at that time the loss of control had to be both sudden and temporary, and driving to someone's house indicates it was neither of these things.*

Task 9 Application practice: Diminished responsibility

Mrs Freaney admitted killing her son so there is no need to discuss the law on murder. She killed with intent so the only issue is whether one of the special defences applies. She pleaded diminished responsibility and this comes under the **Coroners and Justice Act 2009 s 52.** She would first need to show that she was suffering from an 'abnormality of mental functioning' at the time of the killing. Under the old law, in **Byrne 1960**, it was said that 'abnormality of mind' meant a state of mind so different from that of normal human beings that the reasonable man would deem it abnormal. It is likely that abnormality of mental functioning will be interpreted in the same way. The abnormality must arise from (or be caused by) a 'recognised medical condition'. Severe stress is likely to amount to a recognised medical condition, in **Gittens 1984** chronic depression was accepted as such, and this seems similar. The abnormality was therefore caused by a recognised medical condition, namely the severe stress. She will then need to convince the jury that this abnormality of mental functioning, which arose from her stress, substantially impaired her ability to do one of the 3 things set out in **s 52**. These are (a) to understand the nature of her conduct; (b) to form a rational judgment; or (c) to exercise self-control. In **Lloyd 1967,** the court held that substantial did not mean total but the impairment must be more than trivial. She seemed to understand the nature of her conduct, but it is possible she could not form a rational judgment due to the stress. It is also arguable that she was unable to exercise self-control at the time of the killing. The abnormality of mental functioning would appear to have caused, or at least significantly have contributed to, the killing of her son. Her plea of diminished responsibility is likely to succeed under the new law, so she would be convicted of manslaughter not murder.

In the actual case, the jury decided she was suffering under extreme mental stress at the time she strangled her son Glen with a coat belt. Her plea of diminished responsibility was accepted and in July 2011 she was sentenced to a supervision order.

Task 10 Clue spotting – application practice

Phrase from scenario	Focus
Angry at what he said D ...	Loss of control, specifically that it can be triggered by 'things done or said' (**Doughty**)
D thought over what had been said and got very angry, the next day he ...	Loss of control, specifically that it need not be 'sudden' but cannot be a 'considered desire for revenge' (**Evans 2012**)
D had been suffering from severe depression and ...	Diminished responsibility specifically that severe depression is a recognised medical condition (**Gittens**)
D was suffering from severe depression and after several drinks he ...	Diminished responsibility specifically that if D is intoxicated as well as suffering from a recognised illness the jury must ignore the intoxication (**Dietschmann**)
D had suffered years of abuse and one day just 'lost it' and ...	Diminished responsibility and/or loss of control, specifically that long term abuse can amount to a recognised medical condition (**Thornton**) and that loss of control can be triggered by fear of serious violence

Task   **11**

Evaluation practice

The removal of the need for a 'sudden and temporary' loss of control is an improvement in that someone who loses control and waits before acting can now rely on the defence. This applies in particular to abused women, such as in **Thornton** and **Aluwahlia**, who may be physically weaker and liable to even greater abuse if they lose control and fight back at the time. Having said that, it is not clear whether the new law changes much because there is still a need for loss of control to be shown. This goes against the Law Commission's proposals and may prevent the new law extending to cases of abuse against women because any lapse of time may indicate that D did not lose control at all. This seems wrong because it was partly in response to calls for such an extension that the law was changed in the first place. It can also be said that the removal of the rule does not change much in other cases either, because **s 54(4)** now adds that the defence cannot be used where D acts in a 'considered desire for revenge'. There will not be many cases where there is a delay before acting where it can be shown that there was both a loss of control *and* that it was not triggered by revenge. Even though loss of control need not be sudden, in a case like **Ibrams & Gregory**, which failed on this point, any delay could indicate a 'considered desire for revenge' and so still fail because it would be excluded by **s 54(4)**.

The **Coroners and Justice Act** has improved the law in some ways but only addresses a few of the problems highlighted in the Law Commission reports. In particular, it does not take up the suggestion that there should be no need to prove a loss of control, which can be a problem for abused women as discussed above. The new law also makes the defence harder to prove in general, by defining particular triggers and by also providing that where the trigger is something 'done or said' this constituted circumstances of an 'extremely grave character', and caused D to have a 'justifiable' sense of being 'seriously' wronged. In many ways, this is a much stricter law than was the case under the **Homicide Act**. Cases such as **Doughty** would almost certainly not succeed now (although arguably should not have done under the old law either). The exclusion of revenge as a trigger means cases such as **Baillie** and **Ibrams** would fail on this point, and the exclusion of sexual infidelity seems particularly strange, as this is exactly the type of behaviour that so often triggers domestic violence. The original defence of provocation, later brought into the **Homicide Act**, was introduced to protect men who had killed in such circumstances. However, case law may attempt to do justice where the new law has not, as can be seen in **Clinton**, where sexual infidelity was accepted as part of the overall situation so could be taken into account along with the rest of D's circumstances. It cannot be the sole trigger for the killing though.

It is true that diminished responsibility is an alternative defence for women to use in cases of abuse, as was seen in **Thornton** and **Aluwahlia** and it seems right that the effect of years of abuse can be deemed a 'recognised medical condition'. However, diminished responsibility is not really a satisfactory alternative for such women as it indicates they are mentally unbalanced. Women should not have to show they are mentally unstable in order to avoid a murder conviction if their action was triggered by serious violence, even if they had calmed down before doing anything about it. On balance, although the law on loss of control seems to apply equally, in practice it does not because women cannot fight back spontaneously without risking serious harm. Having to use the alternative defence seems unfair. Justice demands real equality of treatment.

The 'fear of serious violence' trigger is an improvement because it includes fear of violence and not just the use of violence. Again, this may improve matters for abused women, subject to the remaining problems discussed above. In other cases, it is a good development because it addresses the 'all-or-nothing' nature of self-defence. If excessive force is used in response to a fear of violence, there may now be a defence of loss of control. In a case like **Martin** where he argued self-defence, the jury were reluctant to accept this defence, quite possibly because if he had succeeded it would have meant he was acquitted. If the loss of control defence were used in cases like this, it could be that it would be more likely to succeed. This would mean that the judge would have discretion in sentencing, but the defendant would not be acquitted of the crime. As murder convictions carry a mandatory life sentence the difference in the effect of the defence succeeding or not is huge: a life sentence or no conviction or sentence at all. The partial defence of loss of control would be a fair compromise.

The new law seems clearer at first glance, mainly because the old law was extremely confusing with a baffling array of words to indicate what might cause the abnormality of mind. However, the new law has not clarified things enough. A 'recognised medical condition' seems to be a simpler formula than previously, but medical evidence is often complex and contradictory, with doctors for both the prosecution and the defence producing conflicting evidence. 'Abnormality of mental functioning' is also still a difficult concept for the jury to understand and old cases such as **Byrne** and **Lloyd** will have to be used to interpret the new law in much the same way as for abnormality of mind.

Abolishing the mandatory life sentence for murder would be controversial because murder is such a serious crime. However, it would perhaps be better because juries are often reluctant to find someone guilty knowing it would mean a life sentence, e.g., in euthanasia cases such as **Gilderdale**. If the judge had discretion, it would avoid the uncertainty of depending on the jury's sympathy – or lack of it – because a jury may convict due to the wickedness of the crime. This can be seen in the case of **Sutcliffe,** where there was clear evidence of an abnormality but the jury convicted him. It would be better if the judge had some discretion as regards the sentence if the jury convicts in contradiction of the evidence. It is especially important in serious crimes that the law is consistent, and judges can rely on the doctrine of precedent to guide future cases, while being allowed some discretion in order to achieve justice in a particular case. The cases of **Inglis** and **Gilderdale** highlight the difficulty in having a mandatory life sentence. The essential facts of these two cases were similar, so the huge contrast in sentencing was out of all proportion.

Appendix: Abbreviations

The following abbreviations are commonly used. You may use them in an examination answer, but write them in full the first time, e.g., write 'actual bodily harm (ABH)' and then after that you can just write 'ABH'.

General

Draft Code – A Criminal Code for England and Wales (Law Commission No. 177), 1989

CCRC Criminal Cases Review Commission

ABH actual bodily harm

GBH grievous bodily harm

D defendant

C claimant

V Victim

CA Court of Appeal

HL House of Lords

SC Supreme Court

Acts

S – section (thus **s 1** Theft Act 1968 refers to section 1 of that Act)

s 1(2) means section 1 subsection 2 of an Act

OAPA – Offences against the Person Act 1861

In cases – these don't need to be written in full

CC (at beginning) chief constable

CC (at end) county council

BC borough council

DC district council

LBC London borough council

AHA Area Health Authority

J Justice

LJ Lord Justice

LCJ Lord Chief Justice

LC Lord Chancellor

AG Attorney General

CPS Crown Prosecution Service

DPP Director of Public Prosecutions

AG Attorney General